921
Mui

Graves, Charles
P.

John Muir   C 1

921
MUIR

Graves, Charles   Col
P.

John Muir   C 1

DATE	BORROWER'S NAME	
APR 1 8 '75	Colombo	16
	R	16

DATE DUE

Colombo '6		
APR 1 8 '75		
17		
JAN 9		
18		
Feb 21 '6		
† 18		
4		
May 27 8 Ⅱ		
20		
May 30 8 o		
20		
Jan 15 87		
GAYLORD		PRINTED IN U.S.A.

JOHN MUIR

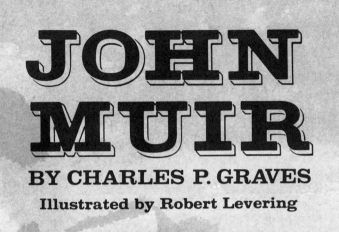

JOHN MUIR

BY CHARLES P. GRAVES

Illustrated by Robert Levering

THOMAS Y. CROWELL COMPANY • NEW YORK

CROWELL BIOGRAPHIES
Edited by Susan Bartlett Weber

JANE ADDAMS *by Gail Faithfull Keller*
MARIAN ANDERSON *by Tobi Tobias*
LEONARD BERNSTEIN *by Molly Cone*
MARTHA BERRY *by Mary Kay Phelan*
WILT CHAMBERLAIN *by Kenneth Rudeen*
CESAR CHAVEZ *by Ruth Franchere*
SAMUEL CLEMENS *by Charles Michael Daugherty*
CHARLES DREW *by Roland Bertol*
FANNIE LOU HAMER *by June Jordan*
FIORELLO LA GUARDIA *by Mervyn Kaufman*
THE MAYO BROTHERS *by Jane Goodsell*
JOHN MUIR *by Charles P. Graves*
GORDON PARKS *by Midge Turk*
THE RINGLING BROTHERS *by Molly Cone*
JACKIE ROBINSON *by Kenneth Rudeen*
ELEANOR ROOSEVELT *by Jane Goodsell*
MARIA TALLCHIEF *by Tobi Tobias*
JIM THORPE *by Thomas Fall*
THE WRIGHT BROTHERS *by Ruth Franchere*
MALCOLM X *by Arnold Adoff*

Manufactured in the United States of America   ISBN 0-690-46412-6   0-690-46413-4 (LB)
Library of Congress Cataloging in Publication Data   Graves, Charles Parlin, 1911-1972. John Muir. SUMMARY: Biography of an explorer, naturalist, writer, founder of the Sierra Club, and early proponent of wilderness preservation who was influential in establishing our national park system. 1. Muir, John, 1838-1914 —Juvenile literature. [1. Muir, John, 1838-1914. 2. Naturalists] I. Title. II. Levering, Robert, illus. QH31.M9G66   574'.092'4 [B] [92]   75-158693   ISBN 0-690-46412-6   ISBN 0-690-46413-4 (lib. bdg.)

1   2   3   4   5   6   7   8   9   10

JOHN MUIR

A CROWELL BIOGRAPHY

When John Muir was three years old, his grandfather often took him on walks in the country. There were many farms in the part of Scotland where they lived.

One day the boy and his grandfather sat down to rest on a haystack. Suddenly, John heard a tiny squeak.

"What's that noise, Grandfather?" he asked.

"I don't hear anything except the wind," the old man said.

"There's something alive in the haystack!" John cried, his blue eyes alert. "I'm going to find out what it is." He began digging into the haystack.

After a few minutes John uncovered a field mouse and six baby mice. He thought he had made a wonderful discovery. He remembered it for the rest of his life.

John's life began on April 21, 1838, when he was born in Dunbar, a little Scottish seaport near Edinburgh. The Muirs lived in a big stone house. On the ground floor John's father had a store. He sold supplies to farmers. Someday he hoped to become a farmer himself, but farm land in Scotland was expensive.

Besides John there were two older girls in the Muir family. When John was three a baby brother, David, was born. Soon afterward the doctor came to vaccinate him.

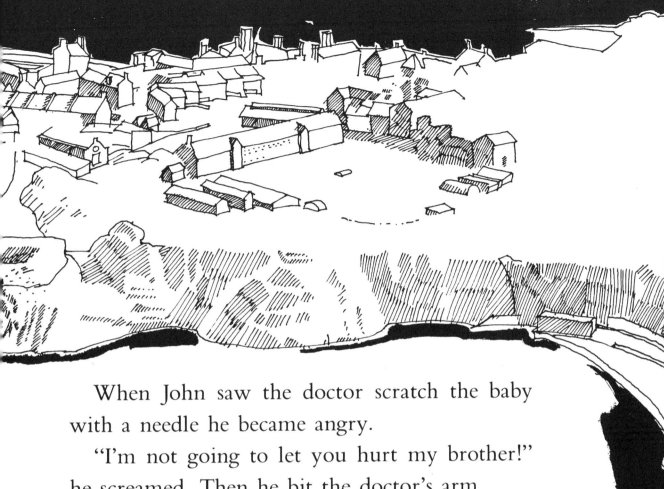

When John saw the doctor scratch the baby with a needle he became angry.

"I'm not going to let you hurt my brother!" he screamed. Then he bit the doctor's arm.

The doctor and John's mother laughed. They told him that the vaccination would keep David from getting sick.

As John and David grew older, they began exploring the shores of the North Sea near their home. They collected shells and seaweed. Sometimes they found eels and crabs that had been trapped among the rocks at low tide.

The boys also played in the ruins of Dunbar Castle, high above the town. The castle had been built a thousand years before to defend Scotland from its enemies. Many battles had been fought around it.

John liked to climb the castle walls. Once a loose stone slipped beneath his feet. John was left hanging by his hands for a few seconds. Then he found a foothold and climbed down safely.

Once a grownup told John that if he were bad he would go to hell. "I'll climb right out," John said.

John liked to climb trees too, and hunt for birds' nests. One day he took a baby lark from its nest, brought it home, and put it in a cage.

The lark seemed unhappy. John decided to let his pet go free. He carried it to a meadow near Dunbar and flung it into the air. The lark flapped its wings and began to sing.

4

In school John read about the birds and forests of America. In those days many people in Scotland went to the United States and Canada to make their homes. Stories about America were popular in Scottish schools.

John learned that much of America was wilderness. Wilderness is land that has never been changed by man. The trees have never been cut down. The earth has never been plowed. The trees grow tall and the bushes thick. John longed to see the American wilderness.

His father wanted to go to America too. He knew that land was cheap there. Maybe he could be a farmer in America.

One night when John was eleven, he and David were studying quietly. Mrs. Muir was sitting in a rocking chair, sewing. Suddenly the boys' father burst into the room.

"Children," he began in an excited voice, "we're going to America!"

John and David slammed their books shut and started dancing around the room. It was the best news they had ever heard.

In the United States John's father bought some land on the shores of a lake in Wisconsin. It was wilderness land and John loved it. On his first day there he spotted a blue jay's nest in a big tree. John climbed the tree to see the green eggs in the nest.

With David by his side, John explored the land his father had bought. They found turtles and frogs and saw foxes, raccoons, deer, and many other wild animals. The land belongs to the animals as much as it does to us, John thought.

One night John gazed in wonder at a meadow near the lake. It was sparkling with thousands of tiny lights. He rubbed his eyes and then looked again.

"Do you see anything strange on the meadow?" he asked David.

Just then a man from a nearby farm came for a visit. The boys asked him about the lights.

"They're just lightning bugs," the man explained. The boys had never heard of lightning bugs before. They ran to the meadow and caught a few of the insects. They put them in a cup and watched them flash on and off.

The older John got the more he liked studying wildlife. But the older he got the harder his father made him work. John labored sixteen hours a day, plowing, planting, and hoeing.

Even in winter he had no rest. His father woke him at six o'clock. Before breakfast John had to feed the livestock, sharpen the axes, and bring wood for the fireplace. After breakfast he chopped wood and built fences.

Since leaving Scotland John had been to school for only two months. His father made him work nearly all the time. When John wasn't working, Mr. Muir insisted that he read the Bible.

"The Bible is the only book human beings can possibly need," he told his son.

John liked the Bible, but he wanted to educate himself by reading many other books. He borrowed some from his neighbors. When his father caught him reading the books, he made John return them at once.

John decided that if he wanted an education he would have to study at a university. But he had almost no money, and his father refused to give him any. John made up his mind to leave home and earn some money.

The University of Wisconsin was in the town of Madison. He went there and got a job addressing letters for a few dollars a week.

John saved all the money he could. Finally, he had enough to pay his way at the university. He had to live on bread, potatoes, and milk most of the time, but he did not mind much. He liked going to classes again.

The other students liked John. One of them gave him his first lesson in botany, which is the science of plants. The student's name was Milton Griswold.

Once when Milton and John were taking a walk, Milton picked a flower from a locust tree.

10

"Do you know what family this tree belongs to?"
he asked.

John stared at the tiny white blossom. "No,"
he said. "I don't know anything about botany."

"Well, no matter," Milton said. "What is this
flower like?"

"It's like a pea flower," John replied.

"You're right," Milton said. "It belongs to the
pea family."

11

Milton went on to explain that, though the locust is a tree, and the pea a vine, they are alike in many ways. From that moment on, John spent much of his spare time studying plants.

John also became interested in geology, or rock science, the study of the earth's history. John learned to tell which rocks had been shaped by glaciers. Glaciers are great fields of moving ice. A million years ago much of North America was buried under glaciers.

When John left the university he wanted to live in the wilderness and study nature. But first he had to earn some money to live on. He got a job making wagon wheels in Indiana.

While at work one day, a sharp tool slipped out of John's hand and pierced his right eye. John was afraid that he would be half-blind all his life. But his eye was not injured as badly as he thought. After resting for several weeks in a dark room he recovered his sight.

John decided that he would never work in a factory again. He wanted to study the plants in the southeastern part of the United States. There were plants there that he had never seen.

Before he started on his trip John went home

to visit his family. He and his father had many arguments. Mr. Muir thought John's interest in plants was a waste of time.

As John got ready to leave, his father asked, "Haven't you forgotten something?"

"I don't think so," John said.

"You have forgotten to pay for your room and meals."

Angrily, John reached in his pocket and pulled out some money. He gave it to his father and said, "I thought I was welcome here. It will be a long time before I come again."

John took a train to Kentucky and then started walking south. As he hiked through the woods he gathered plants and drew sketches of them in his notebook.

In the notebook John also wrote his name and gave his address as "Earth Planet – Universe." At the time that was the only address he had.

John usually spent the night at a farmhouse along the way. But sometimes he camped out. He would light a fire and brew some hot tea. Then he would make a bed out of a pile of leaves.

The Civil War had been over for only a few years. As John hiked through Tennessee and North Carolina, he met many black people who had been slaves. Once when he was hungry a black family

gave him supper. Although they were poor, they shared their cornbread and string beans with the stranger from the North.

John walked a thousand miles. He climbed mountains, crossed rivers, and waded through swamps. He went all the way to Florida and learned much about southern trees and plants.

The trip made John long to see more of America. He had heard that some of the Sierra Nevadas in California were more than twice as high as any mountains in the South. John wanted to see them.

He took a ship to New York City. Then he boarded another ship for San Francisco. From there he started walking toward the mountains.

John was excited when he saw the Sierra Nevadas. They seemed to fill half the sky. It was early spring and the peaks were covered with snow, sparkling in the sunshine.

When John reached Yosemite Valley he looked up at the towering cliffs which almost surround it. Waterfalls, gleaming like silver, leaped from the heights to the valley floor. The valley itself was knee deep with gold and purple wild flowers. John thought it was the most beautiful spot on earth.

He wanted to stay in the valley. Men were building a few small hotels there. They hired John to saw wood.

John refused to cut any living trees. He sawed only the pine trees, oaks, and cedars that had been blown down in storms. He liked the living trees too much to cut them down.

The giant sequoias, which grew near Yosemite Valley, were John's favorite trees. Some of them were three hundred feet high and more than three thousand years old.

When John was not working, he climbed many of the nearby Sierra Nevadas. He carried a pack with his blankets and food. John liked to make oatmeal cakes. He cooked them on his campfire.

John learned how to climb over big rocks without slipping and how to leap safely across streams. With his long beard wagging under his chin, he looked almost like a mountain goat.

18

So that he would not get lost John always carried a compass. He made maps of the mountains he explored.

John liked to breathe the pure mountain air. He often lay on his back and gazed through the fir trees at the cloudless sky. The violets and the giant larkspurs blooming on the mountains filled him with delight.

Quietly he stood and watched butterflies float from flower to flower. He spent hours studying woodpeckers, owls, and hawks.

John's heart always beat faster when he saw deer and bears. But he was also interested in little insects. "A jolly fellow is the grasshopper," he said.

Because he loved the mountains so much, John decided to quit his job and spend all his time exploring them. Other explorers had said that there were no glaciers in California. John proved they were wrong. He dug through what other

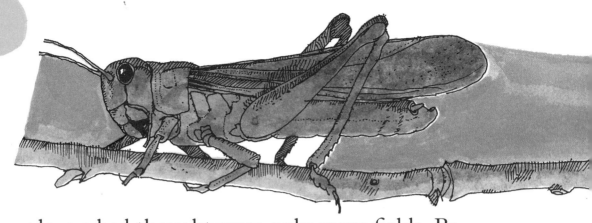

explorers had thought were only snow fields. Beneath the snow he found glacial ice that was slowly moving down the mountains.

In winter John became the caretaker of a hotel in Yosemite Valley. While living there he wrote magazine articles about the mountains. He described the glaciers, trees, flowers, birds, animals, and insects. Many people who read John's articles came to see the mountains.

Once John visited some friends in Oakland, a city near San Francisco. There he met a young woman named Louise Wanda Strentzel. He and Louise were married in the spring of 1880.

Louise's father gave them some land and John became a farmer so he could support his wife.

21

Louise encouraged him to leave the farm every summer. She knew how much he loved the wilderness.

John made several trips to Alaska. The mountains there seem to rise right out of the water. Like giant rivers of ice, the glaciers flow into the sea.

On one trip to Alaska John made friends with a little black dog named Stickeen. The dog was owned by one of the other men on the trip, but he liked John best.

The men camped near the glaciers. The next

morning John got up early to explore. He stuffed some bread in his pockets and quietly left camp.

He had gone only a few yards when Stickeen came bounding after him. John tried to make the dog go back. Stickeen paid no attention.

With the dog barking at his heels John started across a glacier. There were many big cracks in the ice, some of them a thousand feet deep.

John would jump across the cracks and Stickeen would leap after him. A slip meant instant death on the ice below. But the two explorers crossed without mishap.

On the return trip they came to a crack that was too wide to jump over. Luckily, John soon found a bridge of ice that crossed it. But the bridge was twenty-five feet below the level of the glacier.

With the axe he always carried, John cut steps in the ice down to the bridge. After crossing the bridge, he cut steps to the top of the other side.

When John reached safety, he called for Stickeen to follow him. The little dog looked at the bottomless crack and started moaning with fear.

John was worried that Stickeen might slip and fall to his death. But he knew the dog would die of hunger and cold if he stayed on the glacier.

Suddenly, Stickeen stopped moaning and started slowly down the steps. The dog reached the bridge and crossed it. John knew that dogs are poor climbers. Coming up the steps would be the most dangerous part for Stickeen.

The dog stopped for a moment, looking at the steps. All at once he jumped toward them, digging his paws in the ice. When he reached the top he dashed around in circles, barking with relief.

John told the story of Stickeen many times. Later he wrote a book about him.

When John returned to California he planted

24

many grape vines and pear trees on his farm. He wanted to make enough money so that he could stop farming after a time.

Before long the Muirs had two daughters. The girls were named Wanda and Helen.

As soon as they were old enough, John taught them the names of the plants and flowers near the house.

"How would you like it," he often asked, "if people didn't call you by your names?"

As the years went by the Muirs' farm did well. Finally, John had enough money to take care of his family for the rest of their lives. Now he could afford to spend the rest of *his* life studying and writing about nature and the wilderness.

John made another trip through the Sierra Nevadas. He was shocked to see what had happened during the years he had been away. Many of the most beautiful parts were being destroyed.

Lumbermen were cutting down the trees and selling the wood. Even the mighty sequoias were not safe.

"Any fool can destroy trees," John said. "They cannot defend themselves or run away."

The mountains were also being hurt by sheep. Ranchers sent thousands of them to graze in the high meadows. The sheep ate the grass and the wild flowers.

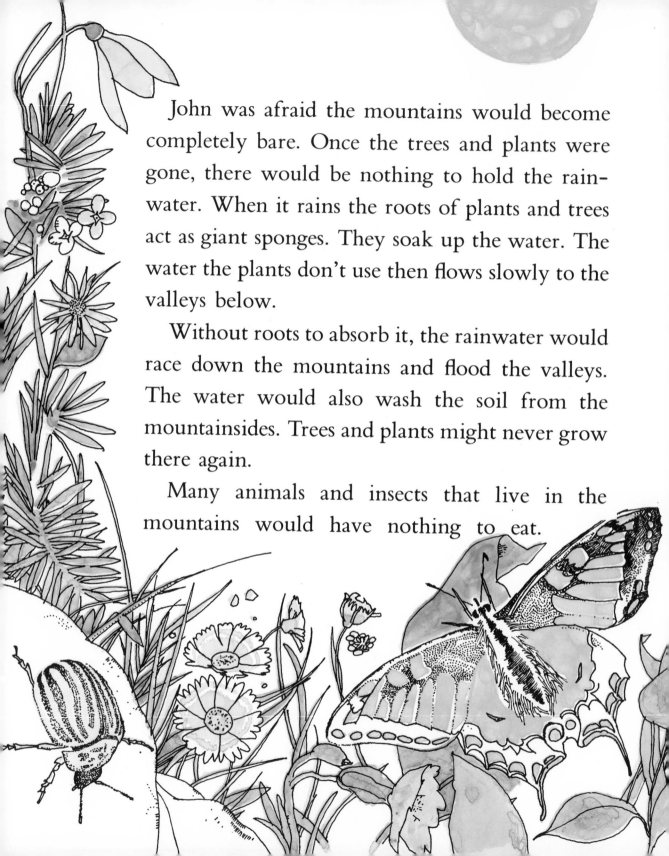

John was afraid the mountains would become completely bare. Once the trees and plants were gone, there would be nothing to hold the rainwater. When it rains the roots of plants and trees act as giant sponges. They soak up the water. The water the plants don't use then flows slowly to the valleys below.

Without roots to absorb it, the rainwater would race down the mountains and flood the valleys. The water would also wash the soil from the mountainsides. Trees and plants might never grow there again.

Many animals and insects that live in the mountains would have nothing to eat.

They would die. The animals that feed on them would die too. Without animals and plants, man could not live either.

"Everything is hitched to everything else," John often said.

This relationship between living things and the places where they live is called ecology. When John was alive, ecology was a brand new science. John had probably never heard the word "ecology," but he knew a great deal about it.

John made up his mind to try to save the California wilderness from the lumbermen and the sheep ranchers. He wanted to keep water from flooding the valleys. Even more than that, he wanted to save the beauty of the mountains.

"Everybody needs beauty as well as bread," John said. He believed that people should have places where they could rest their bodies, lift their spirits, and be at peace with the world.

In 1892 John helped form the Sierra Club. The club wanted to save the Sierra Nevadas for all the people to enjoy. John was president of the club.

He made speeches and wrote magazine articles about the importance of keeping some parts of America wild forever. The United States government owned much of the wilderness land. John finally persuaded the government to set aside parts of it, in other states as well as in California, as national parks.

Yosemite National Park was John's favorite. The wild Hetch Hetchy Valley was in the park. John liked to camp beside the river which ran through it. The water dashed against rocks and splashed high into the air. Above the river a waterfall tumbled from a cliff. John said it looked like a silver scarf.

He was angry when he learned that some people in San Francisco wanted to dam Hetch Hetchy's river. They planned to turn the valley into a lake and pipe the water to the city.

John knew that San Francisco needed water. But he thought the city should get it from another place. John believed it was a crime to destroy part of a national park.

He was an old man now. His hair was as white as the snow on the mountains he loved so much. But he was still strong and full of energy.

John wrote many letters and newspaper stories about the beauty of Hetch Hetchy. He talked to Presidents, Congressmen, and other important people in the government. But in the end, John lost his fight to save the valley.

The defeat almost broke his heart. Soon afterward, in 1914, he died. The beautiful Hetch Hetchy Valley was buried forever under tons of water.

But before John died he had convinced many

people that wilderness lands should be saved. They carried on his work. Today, thanks to John Muir, there are many national parks. Mountain ranges, canyons, seashores, and islands have been made into parks.

Many Americans visit them each year. They hike on forest trails, swim in clear water, and breathe clean mountain air.

John Muir once said that the fight to save the wilderness would go on forever. He called it a war between right and wrong.

Some people would like to make money out of the wilderness areas. They want to build motels, ski runs, and ski lifts in the parks. Other people want to build wide roads through them and airports near them.

Millions of Americans, however, are fighting John Muir's battles. Like him they know that man must save the wilderness in order to save himself.

ABOUT THE AUTHOR

Charles P. Graves has written for advertising agencies and newspapers, and is the author of over twenty-five books for children. He is especially well known for his biographies, among them *John F. Kennedy, Benjamin Franklin, Grandma Moses, Annie Oakley,* and *Mark Twain.*

Mr. Graves grew up in Gainesville, Florida, a town that John Muir described in his first book, *A Thousand Mile Walk to the Gulf.* As a boy, Mr. Graves loved exploring the Florida swamps and sinkholes, and swimming in the wild streams and crystal springs. During World War II, he served with the Ski Troops and trained in the mountains of Colorado. After the war, he lived in California for a time and camped in the High Sierra, where John Muir spent a great part of his life.

Until his recent death, Charles Graves lived in Irvington, New York, with his wife, a children's books editor, and his children, Liza and John. An especially active man, he spent his time gardening, playing tennis, working for the peace movement, and teaching his children sports, when not busy researching and writing his biographies.

ABOUT THE ILLUSTRATOR

As a teen-ager, Robert Levering operated an amateur radio station, studied the classical guitar, played the trumpet and Conga drums, and tried a variety of strenuous summer jobs. Art, however, was always his first love. Today he has had his paintings exhibited in Washington, D.C., and New York City, and he has received repeated recognition for his commercial art.

A native of Ypsilanti, Michigan, Mr. Levering received an A.B. degree from the University of Arizona and studied at several art schools in the Midwest and the East. His travels, for both work and pleasure, have taken him to North Africa, Europe, South America, Mexico, and the Middle East. He lives in New York City.